MLB's Greatest Teams

ATLANTA BRAVES

Caroline Wesley

Big Buddy Books
An Imprint of Abdo Publishing
abdobooks.com

abdobooks.com

Published by Abdo Publishing, a division of ABDO, PO Box 398166, Minneapolis, Minnesota 55439.
Copyright © 2019 by Abdo Consulting Group, Inc. International copyrights reserved in all countries. No part
of this book may be reproduced in any form without written permission from the publisher. Big Buddy Books™
is a trademark and logo of Abdo Publishing.

Printed in the United States of America, North Mankato, Minnesota.
102018
012019

Cover Photo: Kevin C. Cox/Getty Images.
Interior Photos: 33ft/Depositphotos (p. 7); AP Images (pp. 22, 28); Chris Graythen/Getty Images (p. 24);
    Craig Melvin/Getty Images (p. 23); Ed Reinke/AP Images (p. 17); J. Walter Green/AP Images (p. 13); Joe
    McTyre/AP Images (p. 29); Kevin C. Cox/Getty Images (p. 9); Matthew Stockman/Getty Images (pp. 24,
    25); Mike Zarrilli/Getty Images (p. 5); Paul Shane/AP Images (p. 21); Rich Schultz/Getty Images (p. 27);
    Stephen Dunn/Getty Images (p. 19); Tom DiPace/AP Images (p. 23); Tom Sande/AP Images (pp. 11, 15).

Coordinating Series Editor: Tamara L. Britton
Contributing Editor: Jill M. Roesler
Graphic Design: Jenny Christensen, Cody Laberda

Library of Congress Control Number: 2018948451

Publisher's Cataloging-in-Publication Data

Names: Wesley, Caroline, author.
Title: Atlanta Braves / by Caroline Wesley.
Description: Minneapolis, Minnesota : Abdo Publishing, 2019 | Series: MLB's
    greatest teams set 2 | Includes online resources and index.
Identifiers: ISBN 9781532118067 (lib. bdg.) | ISBN 9781532171109 (ebook)
Subjects: LCSH: Atlanta Braves (Baseball team)--Juvenile literature. | Baseball
    teams--United States--History--Juvenile literature. | Major League Baseball
    (Organization)--Juvenile literature. | Baseball--Juvenile literature.
Classification: DDC 796.35764--dc23

Contents

Major League Baseball

League Play

There are two leagues in MLB. They are the American League (AL) and the National League (NL). Each league has 15 teams and is split into three divisions. They are east, central, and west.

The Atlanta Braves is one of 30 Major League Baseball (MLB) teams. The team plays in the National League East **Division**.

Throughout the season, all MLB teams play 162 games. The season begins in April and can continue until November.

The Braves' mascot Blooper joined the team in 2018.

A Winning Team

The Braves team is from Atlanta, Georgia. The team's colors are scarlet, navy, and gold.

The team has had good seasons and bad. But time and again, the Braves players have proven themselves. Let's see what makes the Braves one of MLB's greatest teams!

Fast Facts

HOME FIELD: SunTrust Park

TEAM COLORS: Scarlet, navy, and gold

TEAM SONG:
"The Tomahawk Chop"

PENNANTS: 17

WORLD SERIES TITLES:
1914, 1957, 1995

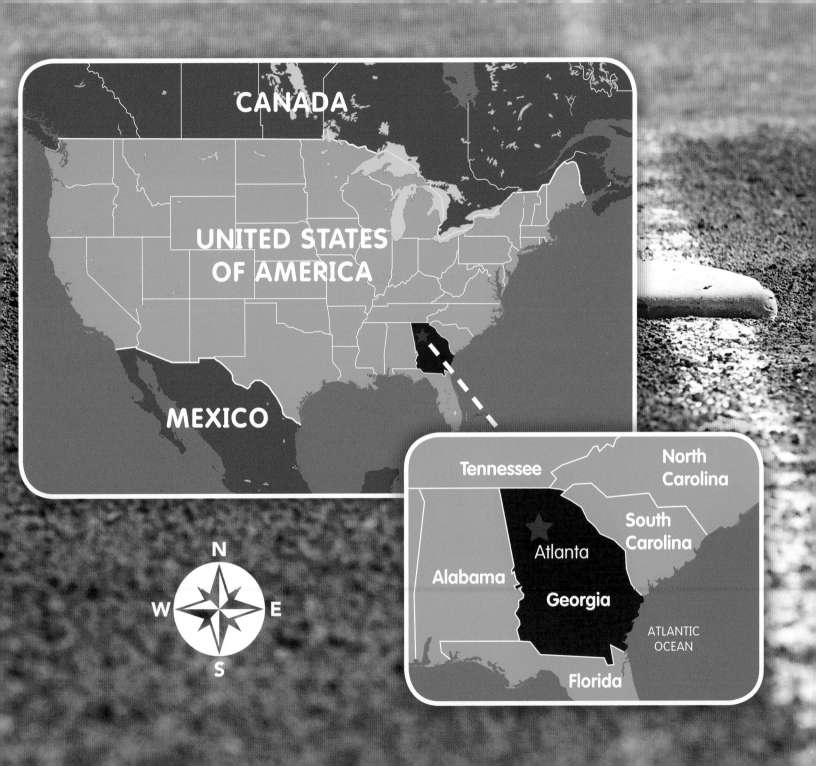

CANADA

UNITED STATES
OF AMERICA

MEXICO

N
W E
S

Tennessee

North
Carolina

South
Carolina

Alabama

Atlanta

Georgia

ATLANTIC
OCEAN

Florida

SunTrust Park

From 1871 to 1953, the Braves played at two different ballparks in Boston, Massachusetts. The team moved to Milwaukee, Wisconsin in 1953. There, it played at the County Stadium.

Finally in 1966, the Braves moved to its current home in Atlanta. Team members played in the Atlanta-Fulton County Stadium for 30 years. From 1997 to 2016, the players competed at Turner Field. And in 2017, the team moved to SunTrust Park.

The Braves' biggest rival is the New York Mets.

Then and Now

The Boston Red Stockings began as a member of the National Association of Professional Base Ball Players in 1871. The team was successful from the start. From 1872 to 1878, the players won six **pennants**.

The team joined the NL in 1876. A few years later, its name changed to the Beaneaters. The team also tried other names such as the Doves and the Rustlers. Finally in 1912, team owners settled on the Braves.

The Braves changed the team name again in 1936. Players competed as the Bees for five years.

The team struggled during the early 1900s. From 1900 to 1913, the team often placed last in its league. Halfway through the 1914 season, second baseman Johnny Evers **encouraged** team members to work harder.

After that, the Braves began winning game after game. By October, the team had shot up to first place in the NL. The Braves won the first four games of the 1914 World Series. They had become World Series **champions**!

During the 1914 season, the team earned the nickname The Miracle Braves.

Highlights

After the 1914 season, the Braves had only 13 winning seasons over the next 40 years. So the team moved to Milwaukee in 1953 for a fresh start. There, the team began placing higher in the league.

The Braves made it to the **playoffs** in 1957. In game seven, the players beat the New York Yankees. The team won its second World Series title!

Babe Ruth *(right)* played with the Braves for 28 games in 1935.

In 1966, the Braves moved to Atlanta. From then until 1990, the team suffered 17 losing seasons. Players made it to the **Championship** Series in 1969 and 1982. But they lost both times.

After many losing seasons, the team began rebuilding. Players collected back-to-back NL **pennants** in 1991 and 1992. Three years later, the team won its third World Series!

The Braves made it to the **playoffs** every year over the next ten years. Players earned five NL **Division** titles, and two more NL pennants.

The top team from each AL and NL division goes to the playoffs. Each league also sends one wild-card team. One team from the AL and one from the NL will win the pennant. The two pennant winners then go to the World Series!

The Braves won four out of six games to earn the 1995 World Series title.

Famous Managers

Bobby Cox began his MLB **career** as a second baseman for the Yankees. After only two years, Cox **retired** as a player. So he began managing the Braves from 1978 to 1981, and again from 1990 to 2010.

Cox led the team to 15 **playoff** appearances and one World Series win. He earned the Manager of the Year Award three times with the Braves. In 2009, Cox posted 2,000 Braves wins. That made him the fourth manager in MLB history to do so.

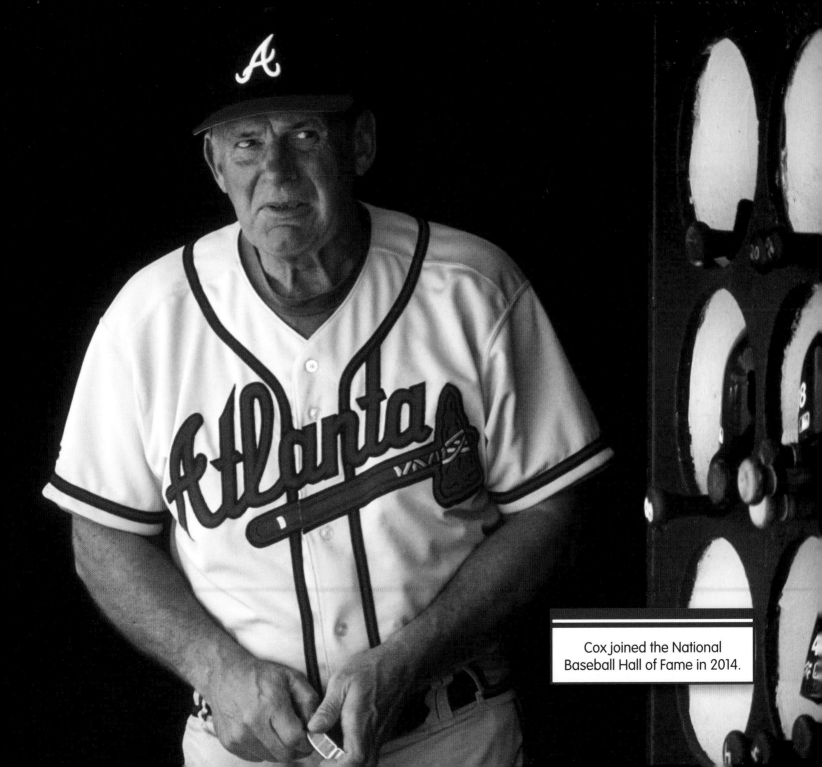

Cox joined the National
Baseball Hall of Fame in 2014.

Fred Haney spent only three-and-a-half years with the Braves. But during that time, he made his mark as an excellent leader.

In his first full year, Haney led the team to the World Series. The Braves won the 1957 Series in seven games against the Yankees. Haney earned an NL Manager of the Year Award for his efforts.

The following year, he helped the Braves win an NL **pennant**. But this time, the Braves lost to the Yankees in the World Series. After the 1959 season, Haney **retired** from MLB.

Haney *(right)* was manager to Braves all-star Hank Aaron *(left)*.

Star Players

Hank Aaron OUTFIELDER, #44

Hank Aaron is an iconic MLB player. As a Braves outfielder, Aaron **putout** more than 5,500 batters. He earned three **Gold Gloves** for his fielding skills. As a batter, he still holds the record for hitting the most **runs batted in (RBIs)**. In 1999, MLB introduced the Hank Aaron Award. The award honors the top batter in each league.

1954 – 1974

Phil Niekro PITCHER, #35

Phil Niekro joined the Braves in 1964. He played with the team for 21 years. Many fans remember Niekro for his knuckleball pitch. During his Braves **career**, Niekro pitched more than 4,600 **innings**. He won five Gold Gloves for pitching. And he joined the National Baseball Hall of Fame in 1997.

1964 – 1983, 1987

Chipper Jones THIRD BASEMAN, #10

Chipper Jones' skills helped the Braves make it to the **playoffs** for 11 straight seasons. As a switch-hitter, Jones could bat from either side of the plate. He earned two NL **Silver Sluggers** for his skills at bat. He also won the 1999 NL **Most Valuable Player (MVP)** Award. Jones was **inducted** into the National Baseball Hall of Fame in 2018.

1993, 1995 – 2012

Greg Maddux PITCHER, #31

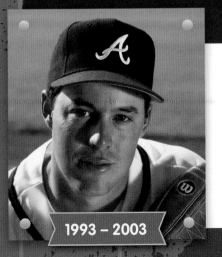

1993 – 2003

Greg Maddux was a very clever pitcher. He was not famous for throwing fastballs. Instead, Maddux threw controlled pitches to **strike out** the batters. In 11 years with the Braves, he struck out nearly 2,000 batters. Throughout his **career**, Maddux earned four Cy Young Awards and 18 **Gold Glove Awards**!

2010 –

Freddie Freeman FIRST BASEMAN, #5

Freddie Freeman is a talented first baseman. In 2012, he was number one in the NL for number of **putouts**. Proving himself a strong first baseman, he began appearing in the field more often. In 2014, he appeared in all 162 regular season games. And in 2018, Freeman was the starting NL first baseman in the All-Star Game.

Julio Teheran PITCHER, #49

Julio Teheran joined the Braves when he was 20 years old. At the time, he was the youngest player in the NL. Just three years later, he joined his first All-Star team. And he played on another All-Star team in 2016. In eight seasons, Teheran has pitched more than 1,100 **innings**.

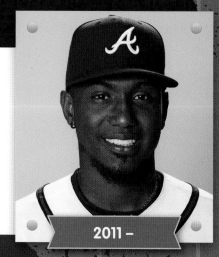

2011 –

Ender Inciarte OUTFIELDER, #11

Ender Inciarte is a top batter. And he is one of the Braves' most powerful runners. In 2017, Inciarte recorded more than 200 hits in one season. This is a feat last accomplished by a Braves player in 1996. By the end of April 2018, Inciarte had 13 **stolen bases**. This broke the Braves' record for most steals by the end of the first month.

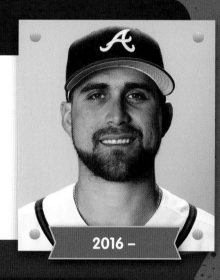

2016 –

Ozzie Albies SECOND BASEMAN, #1

Ozzie Albies signed with the Braves when he was 16. Five years later, he played in his first MLB game. Albies scored 76 runs for his team by August of the 2018 season. This put him in second for most runs scored in the NL. That same year, he made his first appearance in an MLB All-Star Game.

2017 –

25

Final Call

The Braves have a long, rich history. The team has played in 17 World Series, and earned three World Series titles.

Even during losing seasons, true fans have stuck by the players. Many believe the Braves will remain one of the greatest teams in MLB.

Rookie Ronald Acuña Jr. hit more than 25 homers for the Braves in 2018. For that, he earned the August Rookie of the Month Award.

Through the Years

1876
The Boston team played the first game in the new National League.

1893
Kid Nichols pitched the team to its third **pennant** in a row.

1936
The Braves hosted the MLB All-Star Game at Braves Field in Boston.

1965
The Braves led the NL with 196 home runs.

1974

Hank Aaron broke Babe Ruth's home run record when he hit 715 homers.

1977

Braves owner Ted Turner became the team's manager. But he only managed the team for one game!

1990–1991

The Braves ended the 1990 season in last place. But the next season, the team leapt to first place in the NL.

2007

The Braves had more wins than losses each season for 17 straight seasons.

2017

SunTrust Park opened in March 2017. There are 300 pieces of Braves-themed artwork throughout the stadium.

Glossary

career a period of time spent in a certain job.

championship a game, a match, or a race held to find a first-place winner. A champion is the winner of a championship.

division a number of teams grouped together in a sport for competitive purposes.

encourage to make more determined, hopeful, or confident.

Gold Glove Award annually given to the MLB players with the best fielding experience.

induct to officially introduce someone as a member.

inning a division of a baseball game that consists of a turn at bat for each team.

Most Valuable Player (MVP) the player who contributes the most to his or her team's success.

pennant the prize that is awarded to the champions of the two MLB leagues each year.

playoffs a game or series of games to determine a championship or break a tie.

putout an action that causes a batter or runner on the opposite team to be out.

retire to give up one's job.

run batted in (RBI) a run that is scored as a result of a batter's hit, walk, or stolen base.

Silver Slugger Award given every year to the best offensive players in MLB.

stolen base when a base runner safely advances to the next base, usually while the pitcher is pitching the ball to home plate.

strike out an out in baseball that results from a batter getting three strikes during a turn at bat.

Online Resources

Booklinks
NONFICTION NETWORK
FREE! ONLINE NONFICTION RESOURCES

To learn more about the Atlanta Braves, visit **abdobooklinks.com**. These links are routinely monitored and updated to provide the most current information available.

Index